HEROES AND WARRI

Barbarossa

SCOURGE OF EUROPE

BOB STEWART

Plates by JAMES FIELD

Firebird Books

First published in the UK 1988 by Firebird Books
P.O. Box 327, Poole, Dorset BH15 2RG

Distributed in the United States by
Sterling Publishing Co, Inc
2 Park Avenue, New York, NY 10016

Distributed in Australia by
Capricorn Link (Australia) Pty Ltd
P.O. Box 665, Lane Cove, NSW 2066

British Library Cataloguing in Publication Data

Stewart, Bob
 Frederick Barbarossa : Scourge of Europe.
 — (Heroes and warriors).
 1. Frederick, *Holy Roman Emperor* 2. Holy
Roman Empire — Kings and rulers —
Biography 3. Germany — History —
Frederick I, 1152–1190
 I. Title II. Field, James III. Series
 943'.024'0924   DD149

ISBN 1 85314 006 6

Series editor Stuart Booth
Designed by Kathryn S.A. Booth
Typeset by Inforum Ltd, Portsmouth
Colour separations by Kingfisher Facsimile
Colour printed by Riverside Printing (Reading) Ltd
Printed and bound in Great Britain at the Bath Press

Barbarossa

SCOURGE OF EUROPE

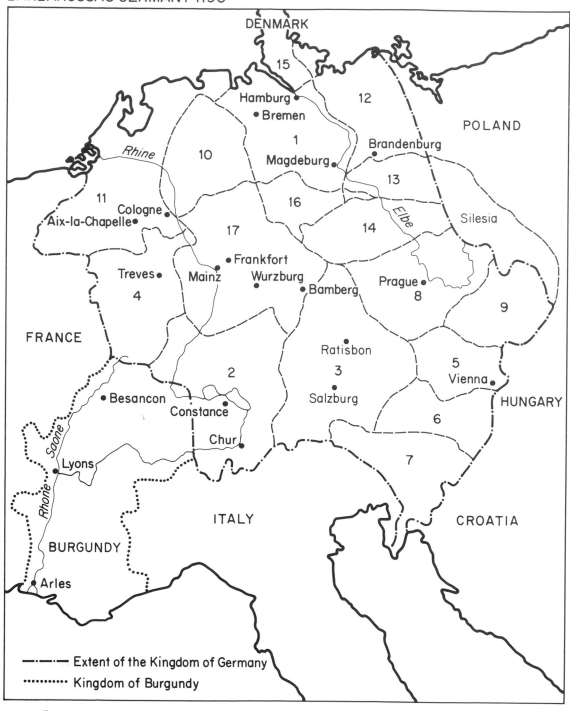

BARBAROSSA'S GERMANY 1190

DENMARK

15

12

POLAND

Hamburg
Bremen

1

Brandenburg

Magdeburg

13

Rhine

10

16

Elbe

Silesia

11

Cologne

14

Aix-la-Chapelle

17

Frankfort

Treves

Mainz

Wurzburg

Prague

4

Bamberg

8

9

FRANCE

2

Ratisbon

3

5

Besancon

Vienna

Constance

Salzburg

HUNGARY

Chur

6

Lyons

7

ITALY

CROATIA

BURGUNDY

Arles

—·—·— Extent of the Kingdom of Germany

··········· Kingdom of Burgundy

- - - - Boundary of the various Duchies within Germany

1	Saxony	7	Carinthia	12	March of Brandenburg
2	Swabia	8	Bohemia	13	March of Lusatia
3	Bavaria	9	Moravia	14	March of Misnia
4	Upper Lorraine	10	Westphalia	15	County of Holstein
5	Austria	11	Lower Lorraine and Duchy of Brabant	16	Landgraviate of Thuringia
6	Styria			17	Franconia (several counties)

Emperor and Legend

The Emperor Frederick I drew his popular names of Barbarossa or Rothbart from his red coloured beard. Born in 1121, son of Frederick, Duke of the German territory of Swabia, he became one of the most powerful and famous of the medieval emperors. In addition to his political and military achievements, Barbarossa acquired a legendary fame; like the British King Arthur, he is said to be sleeping, awaiting the time of greatest need for his return as a national saviour.

Throughout his life, Barbarossa strove vigorously to restore and strengthen the Holy Roman Empire. Much of his energy was spent in repeated feuds with various popes, with the Italian confederacy known as the Lombard League, and with his cousin the other great German prince of the period, Henry the Lion. Despite Barbarossa's will and energy, his plans fell apart immediately upon his sudden death; the tragedy of such an able ruler drowning while on crusade shook the entire system which he strove to uphold.

Barbarossa was, in many ways, the epitome of the feudal emperor or prince: he was physically fit and imposing in appearance, he was skilled in arms and he was a great leader and tactician. He fought many successful campaigns, both in terms of warfare and diplomacy, and most of all he upheld the medieval system of fervent religious belief combined with regal authority. He was also a builder and developer of culture, and worked endlessly to set Germany upon a firm governmental and financial footing after the internal struggles that had long divided the German territories against one another.

This was a period of rapid development in the technology and tactics of warfare; gone were the Frankish troops of the time of Charlemagne, who were expected to be riders, foot soldiers, swordsmen, spearsmen and archers all at once. Specialisation, both within class distinctions and within armed skills, was clearly evident and the rigid feudal pattern of government and loyalty and the honour code of vassalage and service which held the culture together, provided various levels of authority in any army, with ultimate leadership from the king or emperor. Mailed and heavily armed knights were an upper military class, with associated

Knight, mounting his horse, wearing chain mail of the type developed from eastern sources during Barbarossa's reign.

5

servants who undertook the many tasks needed to maintain both knight, horse and arms, before and after a conflict.

Foot soldiers bore the brunt of the fighting, not as the light, multi-purpose troops that the original Frankish warriors had tended to be, but divided into functional roles such as lightly armoured spearsmen or archers. There were also sergeants or armigers who were mounted warriors, upon light horses, with light armour, and of a lower social status than the other mounted fighting men. Above these were the heavily armed cavalry, who were free vassals of noble blood. These were the knights of medieval chivalry so well known through courtly fiction, but based upon historical fact.

In a short study it is impossible to deal in depth with the vastly complex web of politics that surrounded Barbarossa; a glance at the list of popes shows just how complex the situation was; hardly had any pope become established and negotiations opened, than another was taking his place. The religious political factor was merely one of several major recurring problems during Barbarossa's reign, all of which interacted with one another. His entire life was involved with warfare, plots and counter-plots, intrigues, feuds and religious problems. We are fortunate to have a letter from Barbarossa himself, written to his biographer, in which he tells of his campaigns in Italy and of the terrible slaughter that resulted from feuds between the Emperor and the Italian cities.

After his death, Barbarossa became the subject of many legends, including that of the sleeping king waiting to return and save his people. Some examples of these stories are included, collected from German oral tradition in the nineteenth century.

Body armour, prior to the advent of chain mail, as worn by a helmeted knight in a manuscript illustration of the Barbarossa period.

Frederick of the Red Beard

Frederick was a Hohenstaufen, and the second emperor to be crowned from this noble family. The Hohenstaufen were descendants of Frederick of Beuren (died 1094), whose son, another Frederick, built the considerable power and fortune of the family before his death in 1105. The Hohenstaufen castle was near Beuren, in the Goeppingen district, east of Stuttgart.

Frederick of Hohenstaufen had two sons: the younger one became Emperor Conrad III, while his first, Frederick the One-Eyed, was the father of Barbarossa. Because of the repeated use of the name Frederick, it is easiest to identify Frederick Barbarossa by his nickname. The Hohenstaufen family were allied to the Babenburgs, originally from Bamberg in Bavaria. Leopold of Babenburg, who was ruler of the Austrian March, married Agnes, the widow of Frederick of Hohen-

Barbarossa with his sons Henry and Fredrick in the 1188 manuscript from Fulda Abbey.

6

staufen, and they had three sons: Leopold, Henry Jasomirgott and Otto von Freising.

Thus Barbarossa came from a noble family, with a background that suited him to his eventual imperial career. In 1147 he succeeded to the dukedom of Swabia, and within a year he set out to take part in the Second Crusade, under the command of his uncle Conrad III and Louis VII of France.

One of the most illuminating insights into the character of Frederick Barbarossa comes from the descriptions of him in the Fourth Book of Bishop Otto von Freising and from Rahewin, his twelfth-century biographer.

The descriptions are a mixture of quotations from texts which were already known at the time of writing, when Rahewin completed the work of Otto von Freising. These are mixed freely with original descriptive material. The descriptions therefore are also found in earlier works dealing with Theodoric II of the Visigoths, Charlemagne, and other historical characters. The copying of descriptions of famous men from other chronicles is typical of the style of the period, and need not be taken to imply lack of information or plagiarism, for wherever necessary personal details are added. The process is similar to oral tradition, in which good descriptions, tales, or verses are preserved and repeated; indeed the audience or reader would have been disappointed if some of the famous and much loved descriptions were not included.

Apart from the deliberate references to Theodoric and Charlemagne, which are intended to show that Frederick Barbarossa was of the same mould as these great heroes, the description of the Kaiserslauten palace is especially interesting. When examining Barbarossa as a legendary char-

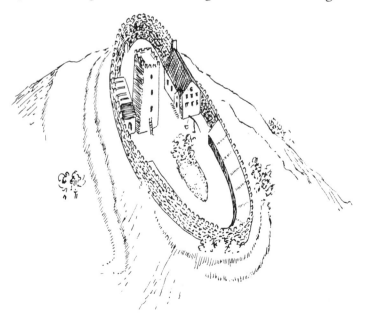

Reconstruction from archaelogical evidence of the original Staufen Castle.

8

acter, this image appears again, from a traditional source collected by the Grimm brothers in the nineteenth century. Apart from the obvious literary currency of descriptions of this sort, it is significant that a garden, palace, or type of paradise is always associated with the sleeping king or emperor, for this is the ancient motif found in classical mythology of the Titan Cronos, ruling in the Golden Age.

Whatever else, the mixture is a fascinating glimpse of the great German ruler:

'Divine august Frederick is in character and appearance such man that he deserves to be studied even by those not in close contact with him. Both God and nature have combined to bestow lavishly upon him the gift of perfect happiness. His character is one that not even those envious of his power can disparage him. His body is well proportioned. He is shorter than the tallest of men, yet taller and more noble than those of middle height. His hair is golden and curls a little above his forehead. His ears are only just covered by his hair above, as the barber, out of respect for the empire, keeps the hair in his head and cheeks short by continual trimming.

'His eyes are sharp and piercing, his nose well formed, his beard reddish, his lips fine and not pulled out of shape by too long a mouth. His entire visage is bright and cheerful. His teeth are even a snow white in colour. The skin of his throat and neck, which is stout but not fat, is milky white and often imbued with the red glow of youth; modesty not anger causes him to blush frequently. His shoulders are broad and he is strongly built. His thighs supported by stocky calves are neat and sturdy.

'His pace is firm and steady, his voice clear, and his entire bearing manly. Because of his shape he has an air of dignity and power, standing or sitting. His health is very good, except that he is sometimes subject to an occasional fever. He is a lover of warfare, but only in the pursuit of peace. He is quick of hand, extremely wise in counsel, merciful to suppliants, and kind to those taken in under his protection.

'You may ask about his daily routine when abroad; he attends matins at church and priestly services either alone or with a small following, and worships so devoutly that he has set an example to all Italians of the honour and reverence that should be paid to bishops and clergy. He shows such a deep respect for divine services that he honours with seemly silence every hour in which psalms are sung to God, nor does anyone dare meanwhile to trouble him with matters of state. When his devotions are over, after the Mass, having been blessed by holy relics, he then dedicates the rest of the morning to the work of government of his empire.

'If he engages in hunting he is foremost in training, assessing, and using horses, dogs, falcons and other hunting birds. He strings his own bow while hunting, takes the arrows, sets and fires them. If you choose what to hit, he will hit whatever you have chosen.

'At meals there is both restraint and royal bounty; moderate drinking prevails without excess, yet those who hunger will never complain of frugality. When it is time for recreation, he sets aside his regal dignity for a moment, and is in such a humour that his condescension cannot be criticised, his severity cannot be called bloodthirsty.

'Towards his household he is not threatening nor is he contemptuous of counsel when offered, nor vindictive when searching out a fault. He earnestly reads the Scriptures and adventures of ancient kings. He usually distributes with his own hands alms to the poor, and carefully divides a tithe of his wealth among the churches and monasteries. He is very eloquent in his mother tongue, but understands Latin more readily than he actually speaks it. He wears his native costume, is neither extravagant or frivolous in his clothing, nor is he ever poorly dressed. It pleases him to have his camp display the signs of Mars rather than those of Venus.

'Though he is famous for the extension of his territories and conquests in which he is constantly engaged, he has also started many public works for the beauty and convenience of the realm; some of these he has completed, and a great part of his wealth is set aside for pious honouring of his ancestors. For he has fittingly restored the most beautiful places built long ago by Charles the Great at Nijmegen and near the village of Ingelheim, adorned with acclaimed workmanship – structures extremely well built but decaying through neglect and age. By this he gives clear evidence of his innate greatness of soul. At Kaiserslauten he built a royal palace of red stone on a lavish scale. On one side it was surrounded by a strong wall, on the other it was washed by a fish pond the size of lake, well stocked with all kinds of fish and game birds, to feast both the eye and the palate. It has close to it a park that provides pasture for a large herd of deer and wild goats. The regal splendour of all these works and their abundance, too great to list further, are well worth seeing.'

Twelfth Century Germany

Frederick Barbarossa's exploits are all the more interesting in the context of the type of society into which he was born. This society moulded many of the ideals, virtues, strengths and weaknesses in his later role as emperor.

German Medieval Culture
Twelfth-century Germany was in a period of expansion; the population was increasing rapidly, agriculture and trade were booming, and towns were growing substantially. During this period, the city of Cologne became the biggest city in Germany, with a population of around 50,000 people by 1180, and extensive trade connections. It also became the

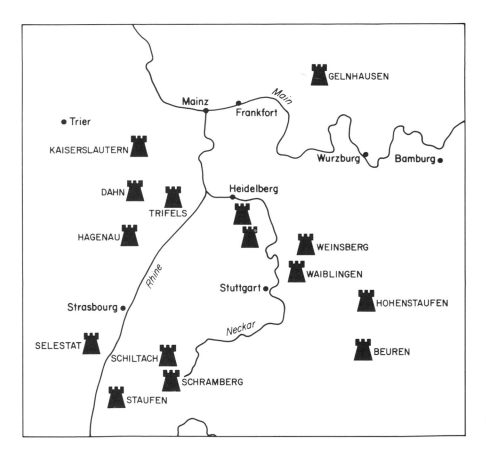

Barbarossa initiated a programme of castle construction in order to strengthen imperial power in Germany.

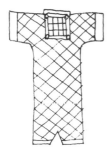

Barbarossa's common soldiers were almost certainly still wearing Norman-style hauberks as late as the Third Crusade.

largest city in Western Europe, with walls enclosing an area of no fewer than 483 acres.

During his youth, Barbarossa saw a rapid increase in the number of monasteries, considerable development of learning, scientific and intellectual skills, and the beginning of cathedral schools, which were soon to blossom into universities. By the end of the twelfth century, there were universities across Europe; at Oxford. Montpelier, Paris, Salerno and Bologna. There were also rapid developments in military techniques, which Barbaross had ample opportunity to employ during his many campaigns.

An important outlet for the growing population, energy and skills of the period were the crusades – religious wars against the Saracens, aiming to free Christian shrines, particularly Jerusalem, from Muslim rule.

Feudal Loyalty

Loyalty to specific lords was an essential aspect of medieval life, running from the most humble serf, who was virtually a possession or slave, to the bond between vassal and lord that held the entire culture together at the highest levels. This is well illustrated by a famous decree made by Barbarossa, in which he ruled that a fire raiser who had taken refuge in a castle must be delivered to justice by those who had sheltered him, but not if he were the lord of the castle-owner, or his vassal, or his kinsman. The feudal bond of duty and loyalty was seen to be almost as strong as, and certainly similar to, the ties of blood relationship.

In contrast to this complex and long-established system, which originally derived from the tribal period in early Celtic and Germanic Europe, we find that certain cities and merchants were freed of feudal ties. Liberties were conferred on cities, in order that feudal laws should not restrict trade and other important aspects of mercantile power. Many cities had rights of self-government, with councils replacing feudal governors. Much of Barbarossa's continual political conflict was connected to administrative matters of this sort.

Feudal service had strict rules, terms and periods, with specific requirements for nobles and serving man alike. The system also perpetuated the concept of the code of honour, in which the strong defended the weak against oppressors, and the highest rulers were always benevolent towards their vassals.

More typical though is this armour from an illustration of around 1190. One warrior wears a helmet with a nasal guard and carries a spear with cross pieces.

The Second Crusade

The Second Crusade was organised by Pope Eugenius III, but was not a success. The planning and organisation were inefficient, and although it was supposedly undertaken as a Christian venture, the Byzantine Emperor Manuel Commenus obstructed the crusade whenever possible.

Newly appointed as Duke of Swabia, Frederick Barbarossa had an opportunity to mix with other nobles, and acquitted himself well in the crusade. His loyalty and courage earned him the friendship and confidence of Emperor Conrad III. He was also able to meet and fight along with his relatives, Otto von Freising, Henry Jasomirgott, Henry, Bishop of Ratisbon, and Vladislav, Duke of Bohemia.

This unfortunate crusade was not a total loss as far as Barbarossa was concerned, for it set the political and feudal scene for his election as Emperor within a short time of his return to Germany. The system of government to which he was elected had an interesting structure and development.

Medieval representation of Frederick Barbarossa as a crusader, the role in which he met his death.

Government of Twelfth-century Germany
The central chain of command and influence was as follows:
The Emperor
Kings and princes
Lesser noble vassals and feudal lords
Special governors and appointees (often placed directly by the Emperor)

THE ADMINISTRATION
Chancellor in Chief of Germany (usually Archbishop of Mainz)
Chancellor in Chief of Italy (usually Archbishop of Cologne)
Chancellor in Chief of Burgundy (usually Archbishop of Besançon)
Administration at county level was undertaken by the feudal lords.

THE COURT
Counsellors
Relatives
Friends and favourites
Court Officials were the Seneschal, Cup-bearer, Marshal and Chamberlain. These were ancient, traditional positions and could be of considerable power depending upon the individuals and the emperor himself.

The Diet represented both central and local authorities, and was a gathering of major importance.

Armour and Weapons

The reign of Frederick Barbarossa saw some important developments in military equipment, particularly in the design of armour. To grasp the overall picture of the weaponry and armour available to the knights and soldiers of Barbarossa's armies, one must summarise the development of equipment during the period concerned, bearing in mind that any changes were not universal and immediate, and that arms and armour of both older and more recent styles would have happily co-existed.

Hand Weapons

Fourteen types of shafted weapons carried by Barbarossa's campaigning armies; military flails (1, 6, 7), marteau (2); battle axe (3), fauchards (4, 8), corcesque (5), military fork (9), halberd (10), partisan (11) and guisarmes (12, 13).

The basic weapons in use from the end of the eleventh century to the end of the twelfth century were the spear or lance, the mace, the bow, the sword and dagger. Variant weapons included the guisarme or fauchard, which persisted in many forms as late as the seventeenth century, and inflicted such horrible wounds that attempts were made to have it banned during the medieval period. The pole-axe was a long-shafted fighting axe requiring the use of both hands, while the standard battle-axe could be wielded single handed. The axe was originally a northern European weapon, and a typical design during the time of Barbarossa would have been a simple axe blade balanced by a spike on its reverse.

Northern European warriors also used the halberd, which consisted of an axe blade balanced by a pick, with the head of the shaft terminating in a long, vicious spike. The halberd was not introduced extensively into England or France until as late as the fourteenth century, but may well have been used by the Germanic troops of Barbarossa, particularly those vassals from the more northerly territories.

Towards the close of the twelfth century the pike was used to counter cavalry charges, and remained in use in various forms until as late as the eighteenth century. It consisted of a long, narrow, steel spear head, with a long wooden shaft reinforced by strips of metal. The butt end of the pike was fitted with an iron shoe which could be grounded to take the shock of a charge, and the metal strips along the shaft (sometimes as much as 20 feet long though usually around 10 feet) acted as protection against sword cuts.

The fork was simply a military development of the agricultural implement. It usually had two or three prongs of deliberately unequal length with hooks added to pull horsemen down, and sometimes barbs. As with a number of shafted weapons, it was used from the eleventh to the seventeenth century. Scaling forks were made with long shafts and prominent hooks to dislodge defenders from walls. The bill was a shafted weapon with a crescent-shaped blade sharpened on the inside; it was current from the ninth century onwards in various forms and, like the fork, had an agricultural origin as an improvised weapon which gradually became specialised in its own right. It was popularly known as the 'brown bill' because such improvised weapons were often rusty. The glaive was another variant of the bill, but its cutting edge was along the convex curve of the blade rather than the concave; this weapon also developed hooks and spurs on the base of the blade for specialist purposes. The glaive was very popular in both France and Germany, and the word 'glaive' was frequently used to mean any knife or blade attached to a shaft.

The morning star or *morgenstern* was a German weapon, used by both cavalry and infantry. The infantry version had a longer shaft, but both versions were essentially spiked maces. The Germanic cavalry often had morning stars made entirely of iron.

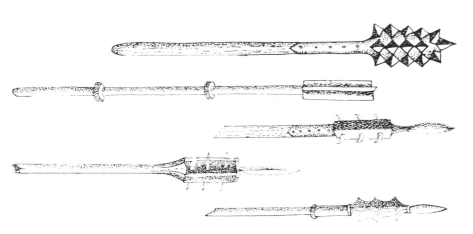

Guisarmes (top) were used to great effect as thrusting and cutting weapons on long shafts whilst (above) the cultellus was used to administer the coup de grace to unhorsed knights, and the war scythe and glaive to pull the horsemen from his saddle. Other hand-held weapons of the time (left) were the morning star or morgenstern, mace and goedendag.

15

Other ferocious hand weapons were the 'holy water sprinklers' or military flails.

A close relative of the *morgenstern* was the aptly named 'holy water sprinkler', more prosaically known as the military flail. This consisted of a long or short shaft with a staple at the end, to which a chain was attached. The chain terminated in an iron ball covered with spikes; a variant form had the chain supporting a wooden or iron flail sprouting spikes.

The mace, or goedendag, was a weapon used throughout Europe up to the sixteenth century. Many variant forms existed, but the basic shape was a central weighted head surrounded by flanges, sometimes with a spike for thrusting. In later centuries the mace was to become an emblem of authority, and is still used by town councils and corporations in Europe as a ceremonial implement. The mace was particularly favoured by militant churchmen, who argued that although the scriptures forbade the shedding of blood, and thus precluded them from wielding swords, the mace was a crushing implement and thus avoided such religious bans altogether.

The *martel de fer* was a type of mace used by both horse and foot soldiers, and was often carried by archers in preference to the sword. It consisted of a shaft with a hammer head, often serrated, and balanced by a pick or blade on the opposite side.

The sword hardly varied in form from the twelfth to the fifteenth century: it generally had a two-edged blade, about 40 inches in length. The quillons were usually straight, but occasionally curved towards the blade; the grip was sometimes double handed and sometimes single; pommels tended to be decorated, particularly those of noblemen and princes.

Other weapons found between approximately 1066 and 1180 include the bisacuta, oucin and besaque, all of which were types of pick used to pierce the joints between the armour plates on a hauberk. Foot soldiers used daggers extensively to disable unhorsed knights; these daggers were known as *cultelli* and occasionally approached the length of a short sword. Guisarmes, mentioned earlier, were also fitted with bells to frighten horses, a fact which emphasises the general style of warfare in which the foot and mounted warriors continually strove to outdo one another. Debate as to the relative merits of foot and horse continued for many centuries, and still exists in an attenuated form in the modern technological army.

Arbalests and Crossbows

Although the crossbow is known to have existed as early as the fourth century, its main use was as a hunting weapon and it was not until the latter part of the twelfth century that it became a major military weapon. However, this was not without some opposition: in 1139 a council presided over by Pope Innocent II banned the crossbow as a barbarous weapon unfit for Christian use, a decision confirmed by Innocent III.

Barbarossa's troops subdue the Roman mob at the time of his coronation. The violent citizens sought to kill or abduct the Pope when Barbarossa refused to pay them an immense bribe.

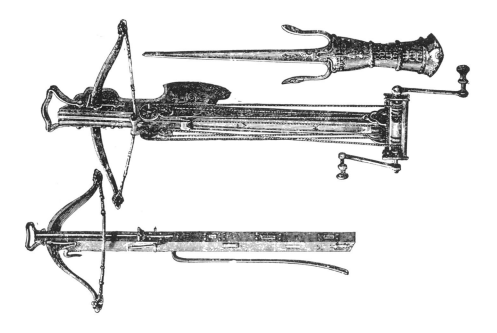

Richard I of England allowed the use of crossbows during the crusade, but in England the famous longbow eventually took precedence. On the Continent the arbalest or crossbow was used extensively, and crossbowmen often formed an individual armoured unit, both for defensive purposes and as a serious threat to charging cavalry.

Hand crossbow, rolling purchase arbalest and Moorish three-pointed dagger; all used on the crusades and during Barbarossa's Italian campaigns.

Early Armour, Shields and Helmets

Body armour varied enormously; earlier forms in the eleventh century tended to be scale armour, in which reinforcement was added to a leather garment. The reinforcements could be bronze, leather, iron, horn, or *cuir-bouilli* which was an extremely hard, boiled and moulded leather. Quilting was another form of body armour, in which the overgarment was padded with wool or cloth sewn between two layers of fabric. This provided a good defence against swords and arrows, but no protection against a lance thrust or a mace. Quilting was also used underneath mail and metal armour, as an additional defence layer and as padding for comfort against chafing. Common foot soldiers, however, often had quilting as their only armour.

Shields lengthened during the period concerned, and the Norman-style long shield, bowed to give extra area and defensive shape, was a standard design. Germanic foot soldiers still used small circular shields, similar to those of their Frankish predecessors.

Helmets were frequently of the standard conical shape, fitted with a nasal strip. The nasal strip was popular until the middle of the twelfth century, when it dropped out of general use. Neck and cheek guards

The crossbowman, or arbalastier, shown here wears helmet and sword of the Moorish influence which appeared in the early 1200s.

Barbarossa was crowned Emperor in Saint Peter's Basilica, declaring that the Pope merely confirmed his existing right to imperial power, but opposed by the Roman citizens and surrounding Italian territories.

The German pot helmet developed rapidly from this basic form.

were also known on helmets, though these were less widespread. The heaume or pot helmet appeared late in the twelfth century, eventually developing into a complete head covering. This type became increasingly common and more ornate in the two following centuries.

The Chain Mail Revolution

By the latter half of the twelfth century, when the crusades were in full swing, chain mail replaced the simpler scale armour to a great extent, and the pot helmet was increasingly used by the wealthier warriors. Chain mail was an eastern technology, and the crude Western version made from bands or rings fared badly when compared to the light, skilfully-made mail of the oriental cavalry during the crusading period. The Saracen warriors were able to ride and fight with far more comfort and freedom than their European adversaries. The best chain mail in the Christian armies was, at first, that looted from the Saracens. A general improvement of European mail occurred due to this influence, but true chain mail was expensive, and the almost exclusive property of the lords and princes.

Germany and Spain were eventually to become major producers of armour: within a century or so of the time of Barbarossa some of the most famous makers of armour were German, while Cologne became renowned for its swords. This last speciality may reflect the much earlier skills of the Franks, the Frankish swords were of such good quality that the Emperor Charlemagne issued an edict that they were not to be exported. Thirteenth- and fourteenth-century German arms and armour, however, were extensively sold all over Europe.

The foot soldiers, however, did not benefit from looted oriental mail, or from the Western revolution in home manufacture. They still used the simpler armour found from the preceding century, with conical helmets padded or plated hauberks or jerkins, and fought with unprotected legs.

Barbarossa's foot soldiers were often still attired like this eleventh-century warrior.

Chain mail was made first by coiling links around a pole and then fully constructed by interlinking.

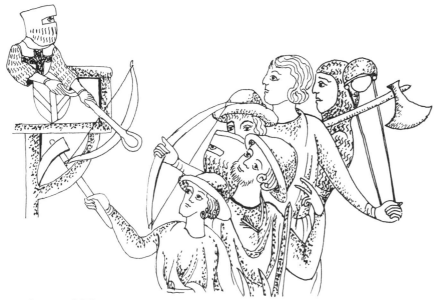

Engines of War

The taking and destroying of fortified towns played a considerable part in the many campaigns and siege warfare of the medieval period. Projectile weapons had been known from Roman times, but much of the technology was redeveloped during the crusades. It may be surprising to discover that medieval war engines were capable of throwing huge objects, and causing extensive destruction within a besieged city. Roman weapons used the bow as their mechanical basis, but the medieval ones tended to use the sling, which made them heavier and more cumbersome.

Slinging siege engines used in the twelfth century had long wooden arms powered by heavy weights. These then developed into the trebuchet, which had a sling at one end of a long wooden arm. Trebuchets had a long range, and were generally constructed on site. In addition to stones, they fired pitch, naphtha, Greek fire, dead horses and other animals, and barrels of putrid, rotting matter. The putrid matter was intended to cause plague in the besieged town or castle.

Although the English savant Roger Bacon deciphered the composition of gunpowder in the thirteenth century, it was used in the twelfth by the Moors in wars in Spain and so was probably known to the troops of Barbarossa, perhaps as a terrible Moorish secret weapon.

In conclusion, it is clear that from this examination of the state of weaponry and warfare throughout the reign of Barbarossa, and given that he lived to the age of 70, he must have experienced many of the gradual changes and improvements in arms and armour that occurred during the twelfth century. Of particular relevance to Barbarossa as Emperor was the use of the chain mail stolen from the Saracens, and the resulting changes in European manufacture that followed.

The trebuchet; a twelfth-century example of this deadly weapon, capable of enormous destruction as a siege engine.

The Emperor's First Plan

In 1152 Emperor Conrad III died at Bamberg. At this time heirs were not selected exclusively through primogeniture, but by election. In any case, Conrad's son Henry, who the nobles had agreed to elect upon his father's death, had himself died. So when Conrad III handed the royal insignia to his nephew Barbarossa upon his death bed, no clearer signal was required of a potential choice, and the German princes, anxious to elect a suitable person of their own choice before any papal interference could be made, chose Frederick Barbarossa. The conflict between nobility, emperor and papacy was to be a constant and powerful factor throughout his reign. Within a few days of his election, Barbarossa was crowned on the 9th March 1152. The ceremony took place in Aachen (Aix-la-Chapelle), the imperial city developed extensively by Charlemagne.

At the time of his election, Barbarossa was aged 28; he was athletic, and excelled in swimming, riding and hunting. He was of medium height, with broad shoulders, and, of course, his famous fair complexion and red beard. Proven as a warrior, he also exemplified many of the feudal virtues so important to his culture and class: loyalty, justice and, where necessary, inflexibility.

It should be clearly stated that Barbarossa was pious; his entire life and style of rule was guided by his religious beliefs. He practised Christian morals, and took a very active role in the development and protection of the Church. However, his complex arguments and bitter feuds with the Holy See were in the realm of politics; kings, emperors and popes were well practised in setting aside or utilising matters of faith and devotion when it came to controlling the apparatus of temporal power.

Most important of all was Barbarossa's inherent intelligence; he was no mere warrior king or religious enthusiast. He understood and developed the concepts of imperial rule and responsibility, and took an intense interest in all matters of law, government and the practical realisation of the feudal ideals which he personally embodied. It was that very intelligence which evolved the master strategies.

Warrior in tegulated, square-plate armour of the late eleventh century.

Shipboard warriors of Barbarossa's army carrying staff slings and fire arrows; a battle axe, spear and sword are also in evidence.

The Revealed Plan

Barbarossa's initial aim was to unify Germany, and settle a number of conflicts which had been weakening the realm. This was to be the first of three stages in a carefully planned development of the imperial role and power.

In 1152, the first plan was revealed by the new emperor. He wrote to various important and powerful persons, including, of course, the pope, Eugenius III, declaring that he would, upon his honour, re-establish the strength and purpose of Germany and the empire. In short, he sought to restore the Holy Roman Empire of Germany, Burgundy and Italy.

In 1153 an agreement of mutual assistance was signed, in which Eugenius III and Barbarossa confirmed support for one another, or more significantly between pope and emperor. Unfortunately, Eugenius died on the 8th July of the same year, and was succeeded by Anastasius IV. The new pope was still pro-imperial, but did not survive for long, dying on the 3rd December 1154. The variations in papal power and support are so crucial to an understanding of Barbarossa's reign that the summary of papal allegiances included is worthy of study and is useful in following the complex developments.

First Italian Campaign

Barbarossa's declared and overall intention was to purify, restore and develop the Holy Roman Empire. Germany was within his immediate control, and Burgundy was the least of the three kingdoms which he resolved to merge firmly together, but Italy was a hotbed of revolt, dissent and major political and economic opposition to his aims. Thus, in October of 1154, Barbarossa mounted his first expedition, with the aim of restoring papal authority where it had been challenged, and fully realising the imperial crown.

He was eventually to undertake six campaigns in Lombardy to subdue and punish rebellious cities, grown rich through the boom in manufacturing and commerce, and increasingly independent of the old feudal authority. The immediate cause of his first campaign was to support the town of Lodi, which had been subject to control by Milan. Barbarossa sent a mandate requiring Milan to give up her claims, but the Milanese consuls tore up the document, and the imperial ambassador fled an enraged crowd.

So in 1154 Barbarossa crossed the Alps with a large army and Milan was severely punished. The city of Tortona, which refused to submit, was burnt to the ground and gradual submission was forced upon all the rebellious cities of northern Italy. In 1155 Barbarossa was crowned with the famous Iron Crown of Lombardy, said to have been made from a nail of the True Cross.

By this time the pro-imperial Pope Anastasius had died, and had been succeeded by the anti-imperial Hadrian. The new pope did not share the

Man-at-arms in the type of armour combining leather and iron developed towards the close of Barbarossa's long life.

21

general goodwill towards Frederick, and wanted to assert the superiority of pope over emperor. While he was not openly aggressive to the strong Barbarossa, he certainly made it clear that he did not wish the emperor to interfere in ecclesiastical matters. Barbarossa, as we have seen, believed it to be his holy duty to weld crown and church together.

A working compromise was reached only after Barbarossa agreed to hold the Pope's bridle and stirrup at a formal meeting; an act of ritual homage which he had at first refused. Meanwhile, the unruly people of Rome, currently opposed to the Pope, suggested that it would suit them better to confirm the imperial crown upon Barbarossa. He replied that he held his power in Italy by the same right of conquest established by Charlemagne and Otto, he had come, he said, 'not to receive as a suppliant the transient favours of an unruly people, but as a prince resolved to claim, if necessary by force of arms, the inheritance of his forebears'.

Thus, on the 18th June 1155, Frederick Barbarossa was finally handed the sword, sceptre and golden crown that declared him fully Emperor, confirmed by military, political and spiritual authority. His first act was to seize possession of the Leonine City in Rome, which came under attack from rebellious Roman citizens based upon the Capitol. But the Emperor and Pope withdrew to Tivoli, where Barbarossa again confirmed papal authority by refusing to accept the keys in his own name. Clearly, he realised that he must uphold the papacy even in the light of Hadrian's opposition to imperial equality.

On 27th July 1155 Barbarossa razed Spoleto, which had paid him tribute earlier in false money. He also put Milan under imperial ban during this period, depriving the powerful city of its regalia and right to mint money or collect tolls. He was gradually moving out of Italy, leaving the Pope to handle his own political problems after an imperial show of strength. But Milan would have to be dealt with again, and Barbarossa would return to quell the troublesome Italians on more than one occasion.

In September of 1155 he finally departed for Germany, to embark upon a further programme of reorganisation in his homeland.

Second Plan – The Great Design

The most important stage of Barbarossa's rule now began to unfold; in this phase he aimed to expand imperial power and to unify Italy, Alsace and Burgundy. His first moves were to settle various internal disputes among his relatives and nobility, ensuring that they were kept satisfied· and willing to fulfil their feudal duty to him as supreme overlord.

In May of 1156, Barbarossa appointed a new chancellor. His choice for this important post was unusual, for the chancellor was not a career diplomat or a member of favoured royal chapel, he was, in the courtly sense of the day, an outsider. His name was Rainald von Dassel, and his appointment was to prove crucial to Barbarossa's success. The imperial system of government was well established by the time Barbarossa came to the throne, with the established chain of command already described.

Rainald was a man of considerable talent; he was described by his friends as being generous, serene and sincere. More important from the governmental viewpoint was that he was extremely active and intelligent, a good speaker and a skilled, astute negotiator. Most important of all was the fact that he was devoted to imperial service; thus his role as chancellor and Barbarossa's role as emperor were seldom to come into conflict.

Barbarossa was ever the pragmatist; despite his ambitions, he paid homage to Pope Alexander III.

23

Although Rainald was a cleric, he did not take his religious vocation with any great seriousness, and on many occasions used his intelligence to give imperial policies an anti-papal effect. He was attracted, though, by ceremony and magical or miraculous powers associated with religion, and when he had the relics of the Three Wise Men brought from Milan to Germany, it was he who carried them into Cologne Cathedral.

Rainald was convinced of divine approval for his role within the imperial cause; his reputation as a soldier was considerable, and he put his skill and courage (which he did not modestly hide) down to the essential 'rightness' of his task. Thus he and Barbarossa were to become close friends as well as working together, for the next ten years. He died in 1167 of plague after the defeat of the army near Tusculum.

Marriage and the Treaty of Benevento

On the 5th June 1156, Frederick Barbarossa married for the second time. His new wife was Beatrice of Burgundy, and the marriage was part of the complex Second Plan to strengthen imperial power. In the twelfth century marriages were generally arranged by parents, guardians or overlords, so this move was quite normal for the time, marriages being primarily matters of finance or territory, rather than of the heart.

Through his marriage to Beatrice, Frederick gained control of Provence and Burgundy entirely, thus strengthening the position of his native Swabia.

Meanwhile, a treaty had been negotiated between Pope Hadrian IV and William I of Sicily (June 1156) in which certain territorial rights were listed, and in return homage and a large yearly tribute were paid to the Pope. This effectively broke the treaty signed between Barbarossa and Pope Eugenius III, and contributed to growing conflict between emperor and papacy.

In August of 1157 Barbarossa invaded Poland to resolve troublesome territorial arguments; and the following month found him holding court at Besançon, one of the imperial centres established by his predecessor Charlemagne. Here the Pope was to further aggravate the already poor relationship between himself and the Emperor. In a complex letter to Frederick, Hadrian implied that the empire was a *beneficium* of the papacy, a gift bestowed only by papal authority. This suggestion was certainly not accepted, and in his reply Frederick Barbarossa made it clear that the empire was independent of the papacy, no matter how closely tied the two entities were through political and religious motives and history.

The reply from Barbarossa, couched in the most vituperative and courtly language, may be summarised by its last section, quoted here from the writings of Otto von Freising, his contemporary chronicler:

And since, through election by the princes, the kingdom and the empire are ours from

Barbarossa's second wife, the Empress Beatrice, depicted on a coin of the period.

God alone, Who at the time of the passion of His Son Christ subjected the world to dominion by the two swords (Luke 22:38) and since the apostle Peter taught this doctrine 'fear God, honour the king' (Peter 2:17) whosoever says that we received the imperial crown as a benefice from the lord pope contradicts the divine ordinance and the doctrine of Peter and is guilty of a lie . . .

Barbarossa's own depiction shows imperial regalia of orb and sceptre.

The Great Design Progresses

By January 1158 Barbarossa was holding a diet at Regensburg to settle internal German disputes. He also sent Rainald von Dassel and Otto von Wittlesbach to Italy as ambassadors. Their task was to take oaths of allegiance from the various semi-independent cities, and to encourage resistance to Milan.

In July of 1158 the Emperor once again led his army into Italy, and by August the troops had reached Milan. With the surrounding countryside devastated, and the common people deprived of all supplies of food, both Brescia and Milan submitted to Frederick's authority, and Milan became an imperial city.

In November of the same year, the important diet of Roncaglia was held, at which all the cities and imperial vassals of Italy were represented. Four of the leading jurists of Bologna were appointed to prepare a document defining for ever the relationship between the empire on one hand and the cities of Italy and imperial vassal on the other. The rights assigned to the empire by these jurists were so great that many cities refused to acknowledge them. Milan prepared for strong resistance to the Roncaglia decrees, which included conceding of all regalia or royal rights to Frederick, such as rents, tolls on roads, rivers, in ports and in market places. The independence of the cities was effectively strangled. As part of the Milanese conspiracy to defy the decrees, a messenger tried unsuccessfully to assassinate Barbarossa in his camp at Lodi in June of 1159.

Death of Hadrian IV

On 1st September 1159, Hadrian IV died. The cardinals, clergy and Roman people were divied into pro- and anti-imperial camps and as a result two competing popes were elected. Frederick supported Victor IV, while his rival, Alexander III, was forced to flee Italy and take refuge in the powerful kingdom of France.

The Razing of Milan

By 1161 Milan was again in revolt, and Barbarossa assembled a large army in Germany, crossed the Alps in the spring, and laid siege to the city. His tactic was to starve the Milanese into submission so the city was encircled by a ring of improvised castles, cutting off communications and supplies. This enabled the Emperor to avoid any pitched battles that would be destructive of manpower, and by 1162 the Milanese were starving and forced into surrender.

It was clear by February that Frederick would allow no compromises; he returned six prisoners to the city, five of whom were blinded, while the sixth had his nose cut off. This last prisoner had been allowed to keep his sight only in order to lead the others home as a terrible example. Milan agreed to accept the Roncaglia decrees, and agreed to the appointment of a *podesta*. Such officials were occasionally native Lombards, but more often were German country squires or minor nobility, proven warriors and trusted servants of Barbarossa. Unfortunately, they often had little experience in civil administration and although the system may have seemed effective in suppressing Lombard leadership, ultimately it acted against Frederick's interests due to its inherent inefficiency and unpopularity. In this case, however, unconditional surrender was now required.

In March of 1162, Milan was razed to the ground by imperial troops, and the inhabitants were forced to settled in four widespread parts of the territory. The city was not rebuilt until 1167. By this dramatic and merciless conquest, Barbarossa pacified northern Italy, placing the territory under an imperial governor.

The Papal Schism

Frederick now attempted to have his approved pope, Victor, recognised by Louis VII of France, and both he and Rainald made speeches at the

Barbarossa ordered the relics of the Three Kings to Germany and installed this costliest shrine in Christendom in Cologne Cathedral.

synod at St Jean-de-Losne declaring that the Emperor had sole authority to decide a papal election. This did not meet with approval, and by 1163 Frederick had returned to Italy with a small band of men, aiming to capture Rome and proceed to Sicily. Meanwhile Alexander III formed a new league of Italian cities from his refuge in France, and fomented further revolts.

In 1164, Victor died at Lucca, and the dubious consecration of Paschal III, soon known as the 'anti-pope', was carried out by Bishop Henry of Liege. This consecration was arranged by Rainald, for blatantly political reasons, and at first Frederick would not accept such an obvious ploy on the part of his chancellor to gain control of papal authority. But the German church now supported the rival Alexander, as they had not been consulted over the appointment of Paschal.

In 1164, Rainald was deprived of the chancellery, but retained his position as Arch-chancellor for Italy. It was in this role that he removed the relics of the Three Wise Men from Milan, and placed them in Cologne Cathedral, where they are still found to this day.

Henry the Lion

The dominance of the figure of Frederick Barbarossa makes it easy to lose sight of other major characters who lived during his reign. One individual who demands special attention is Henry the Lion, leader of the

27

Guelphs. The supporters of Barbarossa became known as Ghibellines from the name of the Hohenstaufen castle, Waiblingen; and the opposition were known as Guelphs, from the Welfs, traditional enemies of the house of Hohenstaufen.

Henry was one of the most remarkable princes of Germany in the twelfth century. Born in 1129, he inherited large territories and an equally large collection of feuds when his father was poisoned in 1139. By 1146 Henry had become ruler of Saxony.

At the diet of princes in Frankfurt (1147) he demanded the return of Bavaria, which had been taken from his father by Emperor Conrad III and bestowed upon an Austrian vassal. Conrad refused, and war broke out between the Guelph faction and the emperor.

In 1152, with the death of Conrad, Germany was deeply divided. The houses of Hohenstaufen (Ghibellines) and Welf (Guelphs) both pressed their claims to the royal crown but as already described, Frederick Barbarossa succeeded in his claim. Despite this rivalry the new Emperor restored Bavaria to Henry in 1154, bringing him to the height of his power as a German prince.

The year 1165 also saw growing unrest in Saxony, where Henry as leader of the Guelphs, had gradually increased his power and field of influence, originally with the encouragement of his imperial overlord Frederick. A strong coalition developed against Henry, including Rainald, Albrecht the Bear, the Landgraf Ludwig of Thuringia, and many lesser vassals from Saxony, Thuringia and Hessen. Thus, internal unrest once again threatened Barbarossa's concept of the great design.

In fact, Henry the Lion ruled territories extending from the Baltic and the North Sea to the Adriatic, but his period of favour and amicable relationship with Barbarossa was not to last long. Those first signs of unrest were found in disputes with various powerful churchmen, who formed a confederacy against him at Merseburg in 1166.

Within two years of overcoming this faction, Henry had divorced his first wife and married Matilda, the daughter of Henry II of England. He then travelled on an expedition to the Holy Land, and in his absence his various enemies, including the Emperor himself, began to encroach upon his territories. By 1174 Henry returned to Germany to serve under his imperial overlord on the fifth campaign in Italy.

In this campaign he led a large body of troops, as befitted such a powerful prince, but due to the continuing disputes between himself and Barbarossa, he abandoned the imperial cause at the siege of Allessandria. As a result of this disloyalty, and his refusal to appear at three imperial diets, he was banished from the empire and his dominions were distributed among other princes and powerful vassals loyal to Barbarossa. After a period of conflict, Henry was forced to accept the ban, and fled to his father-in-law in England.

In 1182, he asked formally for pardon, prostrating himself before

The Hohenstaufen castle of Trifels, one of Barbarossa's family strongholds in the Rhineland.

28

Barbarossa. In return he was promised his hereditary possessions of Luneburg and Brunswick, but ordered to leave Germany for three years, and so returned to England. By 1184 he was back in Germany, ruling his hereditary territories in peace, but with a much reduced status.

However, Barbarossa was still suspicious of the leader of the Guelphs, and when he resolved to go on crusade he ordered that Henry must either follow him to the Holy Land or return to exile in England for a further three years. Henry chose England, but because the imperial promise to preserve his territories was broken, he returned to fight for his hereditary claim in 1189.

Reconciliation eventually followed in the typical feudal manner – through an arranged marriage. Henry's eldest son married Agnes, Barbarossa's niece and the Guelph and Ghibelline feud was thus brought to a close. Henry the Lion died in 1195, and was buried in Brunswick where his tomb still remains.

Oaths and Canonisation

One effect of the increasing difficulties with both papal and civil opposition was that Frederick and Rainald tried to draw the English King Henry II into imperial politics. They sent ambassadors to England to encourage marriage arrangements between two of Henry's daughters and Henry the Lion and one of Barbarossa's sons.

By Whitsun of 1165, Rainald had devised the Wuerzburg Oath. This important oath not only bound Barbarossa never to recognise Alexander as pope, but also bound imperial successors as well as the bishops and princes. Within six weeks all abbots, prelates and vassals were to take the oath. Refusal meant forfeiture of property, and exile. Freemen who failed to swear were to be mutilated and exiled.

On 29th December 1165, Charlemagne, the founder of the Holy Roman Empire, was canonised at Aachen. There had long been resistance to making him a saint due to his open contempt for Christian domestic morality (he had lived with concubines after the death of his last wife). But sufficient purgatorial time was deemed to have passed, and as far as Barbarossa was concerned, it was politically essential to state the unity of the empire and church by accepting Charlemagne into the body of saints at this time.

Revolt in Lombardy

In 1166 Barbarossa assembled his forces to return to Italy, where the rival Pope Alexander had fomented further rebellion. Frederick was determined to capture his papal enemy.

By the spring of 1167, northern Italy was divided between supporters of the empire – the Ghibellines – and defenders of civic independence – the Guelphs.

Frederick put the rebellious cities under imperial ban, and intended to

Barbarossa's imperial seal and signature of authority on a document dated July 1165.

30

IN NOMINE SANCTE ET INDIVIDUE TRINITATIS FRIDERICUS DIVINA FAVENTE CLEMENTIA ROMANORUM IMPERATOR AUGUSTUS

Ratio siquidem et iusticia exigit ut ad protectione et defensione ecclaru dei que p imperium nrm longe lateq; constitute sunt qre nre sola cura extendam maxime quidem ad illas a quib; orationum suffragia die ac nocte percipimus. et si in tabernaculo dei obsequentes aliquid super erogauerimus ab illo uero samaritano cu redierit nobis in centuplu esse reddendum speramus et credimus. Ea ppter cognoscant uniuersi fideles imperii per theutonicum imperium constituti presentes et futuri qd nos intuitu diuine retributionis et pro nra omniuq; parentum nrorum salute dilectum nrm Geboldum uenerabilem abbatem castellensem totamq; eius ecclam monachos et fres ibidem deo seruientes familiam et omnia bona predicto monasterio iuste ptinentia illa uidelicet que dilectus patruus noster heinricus dux austrie pfato monasterio libere et culte et nominatim bona uille que alersbach uulgo dicitur et quecuq; nc habet uel in posteru deo iuuante rationabilit aequirere poterit sub nram imperialem tuicione ac defensione suscepimus. Inde est qd nra imperiali aucto ritate statuentes percipimus ut nullus decetero epc nulla seculari psona uel ecclastica prefatu abbatem uel ei his siue bona eis ptinentia occasione alicui potestatis uel iusticie uiolenter aut iniuste molestare grauare uel inquietare presumat. Siquis aut hoc nrm preceptu ausu temerario infringere presumpserit auri obrizi p pena conponat dimidiu fisco nro et dimidiu predicto abbi et ei eccle hec tamen ut reu maiestatis nre ta diu esse se nouerit donec pdictam copositionem cu integritate persoluerit.

SIGNUM DNI FRIDERICI ROMANOR IMPATORIS INVICTISSIMI

Ego Cristanus aule palacii Impialis Cancellari Recognoui

Acta sut hec Anno dnice Incarn. M.C.Lxv. Indict. xiij.

Regnante dno Frederico Romanor Impatore Victoriosissimo.

Anno Regni ei xiiij. Imperii uero xj. Felicit. Amen.

Dat Ratispone viij. Kl. Julij.

finally suppress the opposition of Milan, Piacenza, Cremona, Mantua, Brescia, Parma, Bergamo and the March of Verona. The result was the formation of the Lombard League, made up of sixteen cities united against the empire. Their aim was to fight for full independence, and to restore Italy to the rights that had been established under Henry V, Lothar III and Barbarossa's immediate predecessor Conrad III.

Between 1168 and 1174, Barbarossa spent what is often termed the middle period of his reign in Germany. He considered some serious reversals of his policies, and declared his son Henry VI King of Germany and King of the Romans. Meanwhile, he attempted to settle the continuing conflict between Henry the Lion and his numerous opponents, which so weakened German unity.

By 1170 further negotiations with Pope Alexander, still in opposition to Frederick, had broken down. It was rumoured that Frederick had attempted to encourage Alexander to crown or at least support the coronation of his son Henry. In return, Henry (but not his father) would agree to recognise Alexander as rightful pope. When Frederick learned of the breakdown of negotiations, while at his court at Fulda in June of 1170, he solemnly repeated his oath never to recognise Alexander.

By 1174 Frederick had led yet another expedition into Italy. However, his princes were not enthusiastic about the project this time and his army was weak, so he was forced to hire roaming mercenaries. These *brabanzonen*, as they were known, were a growing social and political problem at this time and Alexander had even issued a decree forbidding their use. Frederick planned to attack Lombardy from the east and west simultaneously, perhaps remembering the renowned pincer campaigns for which Charlemagne had been famous.

Neither side, however, was particularly willing to enter into serious combat. By Easter of 1175 the Peace of Montebello was partly drawn up, although negotiations collapsed and the war recommenced.

German armour, typical of that worn by the Hohenstaufen knights, on a warrior of about 1100.

Third Plan – and Death

On 29th May 1176 Frederick was defeated at the battle of Lagnano because Henry the Lion, continually striving to increase his own power, had deserted the imperial cause at the last minute. But by 1177 Barbarossa had established the Peace of Venice, which brought agreement between Pope and Emperor. Alexander was escorted to Rome by Christian of Mainz, and Frederick's imperial power was recognised by the various factions.

But conflict with Henry the Lion soon became aggravated; Frederick acquired new territory in Saxony, Thuringia and Lusatia. Henry's failure

During six Italian campaigns, Barbarossa mercilessly razed several cities, including powerful Milan whose population was deliberately dispersed. German foot soldiers acted as engineers, demolishing walls and buildings.

to attend and comply with imperial councils finally led to a declaration of forfeiture of his fiefs, and the title of Duke of Saxony was conferred upon Bernard of Anhalt, the younger of son of Albrecht the Bear.

Hohenstaufen castles had strong, cylindrical keeps, as at Muenzenberg in Hessen.

In 1181 Pope Alexander died and was succeeded by Lucius III, who seemed willing to make compromises with Barbarossa.

By November of that year Henry the Lion had been defeated and banished from Germany for three years. This made it possible for Germany to develop economically and socially, and enabled Barbarossa to consolidate and extend his imperial and personal power throughout the German kingdom. Many new castles were built during this period, particularly in the north.

By May of 1184 Barbarossa was taking further steps against southern Italy, consolidating his hold by negotiation with the new pope, Lucius III. Then Henry VI, Barbarossa's son, and Constance of Sicily were formally engaged, an important dynastic move.

Just as Frederick was gaining increasing power in Italy, and it seemed that the Holy See would become isolated from general support, Lucius died in November of 1185 and the new Pope Urban III, was one of Barbarossa's fiercest opponents. When the marriage of Henry and Constance was solemnised on 27th January 1186, the ceremony was carried out by the Patriarch of Aquileia, who also crowned Henry as

Barbarossa died by drowning or from a heart attack, falling from his horse while crossing the River Salef near Antioch. His sudden death, on the Third Crusade, devastated imperial morale, both political and religious.

Relief portrait of Barbarossa, mounted, whilst crusading to rescue Jerusalem from the Saracens.

King of Italy. This was a direct challenge to Urban, who had not been consulted or even properly informed. A further period of imperial and papal conflict seemed likely.

But by 1187 Urban had died at Ferrara, and within two months, his successor Gregory VIII also died, at Pisa, while on his way to a meeting with Barbarossa. The next pope, Clement III, soon issued a solemn appeal for a crusade. Furthermore, he made real attempts to come to terms with the Emperor, and it seemed likely that the papal imperial conflict would now be resolved.

By March of 1188, Frederick seemed finally to have defeated his opponents on the major domestic and imperial fronts. In the summer he made his last will, and assembled a vast army to take Jerusalem from the great Saracen leader Saladin.

Jerusalem and Death

In May of 1189 an army of 20,000 men was assembled at Ratisbon. It was the largest force that Barbarossa had ever led, and was made up of experienced warriors, loyal princes and vassals, the epitome of the feudal army under its divinely appointed emperor. On 11th May, the many battalions, each comprising 500 men, left Ratisbon in great pomp and splendour.

Frederick first led the army successfully into Syria, and took the city of Iconium. He then moved on into Armenia, but on 10th June 1190, while

34

crossing the River Salef, his horse shied suddenly and Barbarossa fell and disappeared beneath the swiftly flowing waters. His lifeless body was eventually taken from the river.

Thus, while at the peak of his long and difficult reign, and while engaged upon an ideal cause that represented all that he stood for in terms of imperial and religious aims, Frederick Barbarossa probably died from what we would now recognise as a massive heart failure. Despite his arrogance and cruelty towards opponents, he had been a remarkably enlightened and often liberal and generous ruler. Perhaps it is not surprising that he became the subject of legend, his noble image inspiring the collective imagination to attach magical tales to his historical person.

Aftermath

The drowning of Barbarossa was a terrible blow to his immediate followers, and to Germany as a whole. A small party of his vassals took his body to nearby Antioch, where he was buried in the cathedral.

It may be difficult for the modern reader to grasp the emotional effect of his passing upon his people. Such a sudden death, while engaged upon a religious war, and without the essential last sacrament, seemed almost to be an impossibility, an event which flew in the face of all religion, order and concepts of essential rightness. What of his soul? Would he go to heaven, as he had been engaged upon a holy war, or would his sins, unforgiven, weigh against him? These questions were utterly demoralising to the vassals of the late Emperor, and were to cause debate and confusion for many years to come.

Barbarossa's death by drowning as described around 1250 in the Gotha manuscript of the Saxon Chronicle.

Consequently, after Frederick's burial, some of his followers were so
devastated that they committed suicide. Others, and this is most telling
in the religious context, abandoned Christianity and became Muslims.
They felt that with the Emperor's death, their Christian God had
deserted them, or had proven incomprehensibly capricious; or more
positively they felt that Allah suddenly was shown to be more powerful
and in the right.

A body of men under Duke Frederick of Swabia proceeded to Acre to
lay siege as planned, but the effort was half-hearted, and the arrival in
strength of English and French forces by sea removed the Germans from
the forefront of the crusade. Duke Frederick died of disease soon after.

The Succession

Before leaving for the crusade, Barbarossa had installed his son Henry as
regent and upon hearing the news of his father's death, Henry succeeded
to the imperial throne. However, his reign was to be a short one, for in
1191 he contracted a serious illness, and six years later he died.

Henry VI was not of the same calibre as his father. He blindly pursued
established policies and fought to preserve his heritage of power, making

36

little attempt to formulate new policies, and often taking cruel measures to enforce those already in existence. As with the reign of Charlemagne some 300 years earlier, we find that the death of a powerful and talented emperor takes the empire into the shadows also.

Following the proposals outlined in Barbarossa's third plan, Henry VI attempted to make the monarchy entirely hereditary, doing away with the elective powers of the princes. Despite offering similar hereditary rights to the nobles themslves, Henry was not successful in implementing this plan, but he died before any firm rejection of his proposals was made by the German princes. His only son was an infant, and his brother Phillip had to face a claim to the crown by Otto, son of Henry the Lion. Thus, Frederick II, grandson of Frederick Barbarossa, ruled in Sicily and fought to extend his power into northern Italy, but never ruled in Germany in the manner of his illustrious forebear. The final blow to Barbarossa's original plan to restore the Holy Roman Empire, extend it, and give the emperor equal or superior rights to the pope, came when Innocent III became pope. After the death of Henry VI, Innocent took advantage of the continuing civil war in Germany to undo any of the advances that Frederick Barbarossa had gained over the papal power. Although legend persisted regarding Barbarossa, by the beginning of the thirteenth century, within a decade of his death, his historical achievements had virtually vanished.

The Sleeping Emperor

Some time after the death of Barbarossa, various legends became associated with his name. There is some evidence that these were originally connected to his grandson Frederick II, and that by the

Legendary in concept, this depiction of Barbarossa at Gelnhausen portrays him in the company of mythical beasts.

mysterious process of collective imagination and tradition, they became drawn to the more powerful figure of Barbarossa.

What is certain is that he carried the legend of a king or emperor waiting to be reborn for several centuries, just as the British King Arthur has done. We may consider this legend on three levels: nationalistic, poetic or dreamlike, and mythical.

The first level is the most obvious: the sleeping Barbarossa and his knights represent that upsurge of Germanic nationalism and imperialism which occurs in every century. In this sense he is symbolic of the nationalistic cause, either to restore Germany to her former glories, or to justify and inspire territorial ambitions. Within folklore it is always the first theme, that of restoration, which occurs. The more political and propagandist elements are absent from tradition.

The second level, that of poetic or dream symbolism, is inherent in all folk-tales, traditions and motifs of regeneration. Here Barbarossa represents the redress of wrongs, the cure of ills, the great king who will return to bring a new golden age. This leads in turn to the third and deepest level of the motif, the mythical aspect. In this last context we find, curiously, the most ancient and primal root of the entire theme of the sleeping king. He is a representation or manifestation of the Titan Cronos, giant ruler of a distant Golden Age and paradisal land, said to be sleeping in the Otherworld, awaiting a final time of awakening.

Quite why this theme should be attached to Barbarossa in particular is not immediately clear; it would be equally valid, and perhaps more apt, if it were told of Charlemagne. Perhaps it was attached to the great Frankish emperor originally, for one variant of the tale names the sleeping king as 'Charles'. It may be that the curiosity of Frederick I having a red beard has caused him to remain in the popular imagination: red-headed men and women have many superstitions attached to them, particularly red-headed kings.

Those then are the general themes of Barbarossa as a legendary character. The following four German folktales relating to this theme, as collected by the Grimm brothers in the nineteenth century, are typical but only a fraction of the many variants known.

The Missing Emperor

The Emperor Frederick was excommunicated by the Pope; he was not allowed to enter churches and no priest would celebrate Mass for him. Just before Easter, when everyone was preparing to celebrate the great festival, the emperor went out hunting to be away from the festivity. Nobody knew what was really in his heart and mind.

He put on exquisite robes that had come as a gift from distant India, and took of vial of scented water, then mounted upon his noble steed. Only a small number of men accompanied him into the forest. Suddenly, he held up a wondrous ring upon his finger, and vanished from sight.

The Emperor was never seen again. Where he went, if he lost his life in the forest, if he was ripped apart by savage beasts, or if he was still alive, no one knew. Yet old farmers say that Frederick does still live, and that he occasionally appears disguised as a pilgrim. Furthermore, he proclaimed that he would one day rule again over the Roman Empire, that he would vex dishonest priests, and that he would not cease from battle until the Holy Land was delivered into Christian hands. Only then would he hang the burden of his shield upon a withered branch.

Barbarossa in Mount Kyffhausen

Many legends are told of Barbarossa; it is said that he is not dead, that no true Emperor has ruled since his reign, and that he lives on until the Day of Judgement. Until that time, he will remain hidden in Mount Kyffhausen. When he finally emerges, he will hang his shield on a leafless tree, which will sprout green leaves, and a better age will begin.

Occasionally, he talks to people who enter the mountain, though at other times he can be encountered outside. He usually sits upon a bench at a round stone table, resting his head in his hands, sleeping. He nods his head and blinks his eyes with sleep. His red beard has grown very long, right through the stone table; when it has encircled the table three times it will be the time of awakening. It has now circled the stone table twice.

In the year 1669, a peasant was taking grain from Reblingen to Nordhausen. Along the route he was stopped by a dwarf and led into the mountain, where he was told to empty his grain sacks and fill them with gold. He saw Barbarossa sitting there motionless.

Also a shepherd, who was whistling a tune that the emperor liked, was led into the mountain by a dwarf. The emperor rose as he approached and asked him 'Are the ravens still flying around the mountain?' The shepherd answered that they were, and the emperor cried 'Now I am going to have to sleep for another hundred years!'

The Shepherd on Mount Kyffhausen

Many people say that near Frankenhausen in Thuringia is a mountain in which Frederick Barbarossa may be found . . . he has been seen there many times.

A shepherd who kept his flock upon the side of the mountain and knew the legend, began one day to play upon his bagpipes. When he thought that he had fulfilled his duty well, he called out in a loud voice: 'Emperor Frederick this tune is presented to you!' The Emperor suddenly appeared and said 'May God greet thee, little man. May I ask in whose honour you were playing those pipes?'

'I played for Emperor Frederick', answered the shepherd.

'If thou hast done so', said the Emperor, 'Come with me, and thou wilt be rewarded for thy playing'.

Relief carving of Barbarossa as Emperor, in the cloisters of St Zeno Convent.

39

Copper bust of Barbarossa from the Klosterkirche, Kappenburg.

'But I dare not leave my sheep', cried the shepherd. 'Follow me and no harm will come to thy sheep', the Emperor replied, and taking him by the hand led him into a cave in the side of the mountain. They came to an iron door that immediately opened onto a marvellous hall where many servants paid honour to the shepherd.

Emperor Frederick showed him great kindness and asked what reward he wanted for playing so well upon the bagpipes. The shepherd replied 'None'.

'Go', said Barbarossa, 'And take one of the supporting feet from my golden cask as your payment'. The shepherd did as he was ordered, and was ready to leave, when the Emperor started showing him many wondrous weapons, armour, swords, and muskets. He told the shepherd to tell his own people that he would use these weapons to regain the Holy Sepulchre. Then he allowed his guest to leave.

The following day the shepherd took the golden cask foot to a goldsmith, who confirmed that it was genuine gold and bought it immediately.

The most spectacular and dramatic image of Barbarossa in his legendary role of Sleeping Emperor occurs in the Kyffhausen monument.

Barbarossa in Kaiserslautern

Many people claim that Frederick was imprisoned by the Turks, and that

40

after his release he returned to Kaiserslautern and lived there for a long time. He is said to have built his palace next to a beautiful lake, now called Emperor's Lake. He is also said to have caught a huge carp there, and to commemorate this event he took a gold ring from his finger and wore it ever after as an earring. It is believed that this giant carp is still within the lake, and will not be caught until Frederick reigns again.

When people still fished in the lake two carp were caught joined together with golden chain around their necks. This event has been carved on Metzler Gate in Kaiserslautern for as long as people can remember.

Not far from the palace a fine zoological garden was built so that the Emperor could view all kinds of wonderful animals from his window. It has long since been turned into a pond and moat.

Frederick's bed is said to be still in the palace, hanging from iron chains. Although this bed is neatly made in the evenings, it is found disturbed again every morning, as if someone sleeps in it each night.

There is a cliff in Kaiserslautern which holds a cave so deep and mysterious that no one has discovered its bottom. Tradition says that Emperor Frederick, who was missing, lives there. A man once attempted to descend into the cave on a long rope tied at the surface to a bell. He could ring the bell when he could descend no further. Reaching the bottom he saw the Emperor Frederick with a long beard, sitting on a golden throne. The Emperor spoke to him and said that as long as he did not speak to anyone in that underground place, nothing would happen to him. He should also tell his master whatever he had seen. The adventurer looked about him, and saw a wide beautiful lawn on which many people stood around the Emperor. Finally, he rang his bell and was pulled up unharmed to the surface, where he delivered the emperor's words to his master.

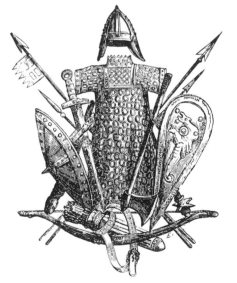

Barbarossa's Letter to Otto, Bishop of Freising (1157)

Frederick, by God's grace emperor of the Romans august forever, sends his regards and every good wish to his beloved uncle Otto, Bishop of Freising.

We have received with great joy the Chronicle, sent to us through your love, which you in your wisdom have complied, or rather brought into harmony things obscured by neglect. [This was the chronicle known as *The Two Cities* written by Otto between 1143 and 1147].

After the sweat of war we ardently desire to occasionally delight ourselves therein and be instructed in the virtues by the magnificent achievements of the emperors. But we would be pleased to commend to your attention an account, briefly compiled according to your own request, of the deeds performed by us since coming to the throne, save that by comparision to former deeds accomplished by better men they may be called the shadow rather than the reality of events. However, since your brilliant mental powers can exalt that which is insignificant and write greatly from small materials, we put more confidence in your praises than in our personal merits, and undertake to outline what little we have done in the Roman world during the past five years.

After we were anointed at Aachen, receiving the crown of the German realm, we held a general assembly at Merseburg on Whitsunday. There the Danish King Peter came as summoned to our assembly, and after pledging allegiance and fealty to us, received the crown of his realm from our hands.

Then we transferred Wichmann bishop of Zeitz to the archbishopric of Magdeburg; and though many disputes and arguments between ourself and the Roman Church resulted from this act, finally apostolic authority confirmed our laudable decision.

After this we commenced our Roman expedition and entered Lombardy in force. Because this land, due to the long absence of the emperors, had become proud, and, knowing its strength and becoming rebellious, we were angry and destroyed most of its strongholds not by the just and righteous wrath of our knights, but by the lower ranks.

The cunning and proud Milanese swore falsely to us promising much money, if we would grant them lordship over Como and Lodi. But as they could persuade us neither by praise or bribery, upon our arrival in their land they forsook their own fruitful country and led us for three days in the wilderness until finally, in opposition to their desires, we pitched camp about one German mile from Milan itself. As we demanded supplies for the army and they refused to furnish such supplies, we had their finest fortress, Rosate, which held five hundred armed men, taken and destroyed by fire. After this our soldiers advanced to the gate of Milan and wounded many and took large numbers of captives. With hostilities ensuing generally, we crossed the river Ticino near Novara and took forced possession of two bridges defended by towers. After our entire army had crossed, we had these bridges destroyed. Next we destroyed three of their strongest fortresses, namely, Momo, Galliate, and Trecate. After celebrating the birthday of our Lord with great joy, we marched through Vercelli and Turin and crossed the river Po.

We next destroyed Chieri, which was a large and well fortified town. We laid waste the city of Asti by fire. Then we besieged Tortona, a city superbly fortified by both art and nature. After three days we reduced the outer fortifications and might have captured the citadel itself, had not nightfall and a severe storm prevented us. Finally, after many assaults, much bloodshed, lamentable slaughter of our foes, and great losses to our own men, the city capitulated; we freed a certain leader of the Greeks who had been taken captive by Marchese Malaspina.

When Tortona was finally destroyed, the people of Pavia requested us to their city to give us a glorious triumph after the victory. We spent three days there, wearing the crown and receiving the maximum acclaim and respect of the populace. Then we advanced straight through Lombardy, Romagna, and Tuscany, and so reached Sutri. There the lord Pope, with the complete Roman Church, met us with joy, paternally offered us holy consecration, and complained to us of the injuries which he had suffered at the hands of the Roman people.

So we came to Rome, advancing daily together, lodging together, and exchanging genial conversation. The Romans sent messengers to us demanding a huge sum of money in exchange for their loyalty and submission, and also three sworn guarantees. Therefore we took counsel with the lord Pope and his cardinals. Since we were unwilling to buy the imperial title and were under no obligation to swear oaths to the rabble, in order to evade their treachery and stratagems the greater portion of our army, under the guidance of Cardinal Octavian, entered by night through a small gate near St Peter's, and so had already occupied the monastery of St Peter when we arrived.

When day dawned, the lord Pope and the entire church preceded us to the Basilica of St Peter and bade us welcome with a magnificent procession beginning at the steps. After celebrating Mass at the altar of Peter and Paul in honour of the Holy Virgin Mary, for it was Sunday, the Pope lavishly bestowed upon my head the blessing of the crown and of the Roman empire. After this had been duly carried out, while we returned to our camp exhausted by the effort and the heat and were taking food, the Roman people dashed forth from the Tiber bridge attempting to capture the Pope in the monastery of St Peter, and killing two of our servants and despoiling the cardinals.

We heard the uproar from our position beyond the walls, and hastened fully armed into the city. All that day we fought the Romans, killing almost a thousand of them and throwing them into the River Tiber, leading off captives, until night finally separated us from them.

When day dawned, our food supplies had failed, so we withdrew, taking with us the pope and cardinals, rejoicing in triumph over our victory. After all the fortifications around the City had surrendered to us, we came to Albano and remained there with the Pope for several days. From there we travelled to Spoleto, and because of its defiance in holding captive Count Guido Guarra and our other messengers, we assaulted

43

that city. The judgement of God is marvellous and inscrutable! Fighting from the third to the ninth hour of the day, we took by storm, which is, by fire and sword, this most strongly fortified of cities with almost a hundred towers. After plundering booty beyond measure and burning even more in the flames, we utterly razed the city.

Turning from there to Ancona, we met with Palaelogus, the noble Greek prince, and Maroducas his associate, with other envoys from Constantinople. They solemnly vowed to us an enormous sum of money as incitement to enter Apulia and undertake by our might and power the downfall of William, who was enemy to both empires. But our army had been much weakened by its many hardships and campaigns, and our leaders decided to return home rather than go down into Apulia.

As we were returning and the Greek forces were advancing into Apulia, self-confident in their numbers and rich treasure, Palaelogus died after taking Bari and razing its fortifications. William collected an army, and made a sudden attack upon the Greeks, taking a few captive, killing all the rest, and carrying off all the treasure. But we arrived safely at Verona with a great victory offered us by God – such a victory as we have never before heard of being gained by only eighteen hundred soldiers. How they laid a trap for us on the steep slopes of a certain mountain, and how they were slain by us and twelve of them hanged, you have already heard. Furthermore, you know in turn the accord we made between your own brother the duke of Austria, and the duke of Bavaria, and how gloriously we elevated Frederick to the archbishopric of Cologne.

These few events, set forth in brief words, we offer to your famous skill to be amplified and enhanced.

Papal Allegiances

(Major figures are indicated in **bold** type)

Eugenius III *dies 8.7.1153* pro-imperial
Anastasius IV *dies 3.12.1154* pro-imperial
Hadrian (Nicolas Brakespear) *1154–1159 dies 1.9.1159* anti-imperial
Victor (Octavian) *1159–1164 dies April 1164* pro-imperial
Alexander III (Roland) *1159–1181 (in exile)* anti-imperial
Paschal III (Guido of Cremo) *1164 (the 'anti-pope')* pro-imperial
Kalixt III *1168–1178* pro-imperial
Innozenz III *1179–1180* pro-imperial
Lucius III *1181–1185*
Urban III (Uberto Crivelli) *1185–1187* strongly anti-imperial
Gregor VIII *1187*
CLEMENS *1187–1191*

Barbarossa was crowned Emperor Frederick I by the Pope. Despite their spiritual office, medieval popes were totally involved in secular politics, holding court in costume and pontifical regalia which expressed their great power.

Cologne Cathedral today. This great medieval church still holds the shrine of the Three Wise Men, taken there by Barbarossa's Chancellor Rainald von Dassell.

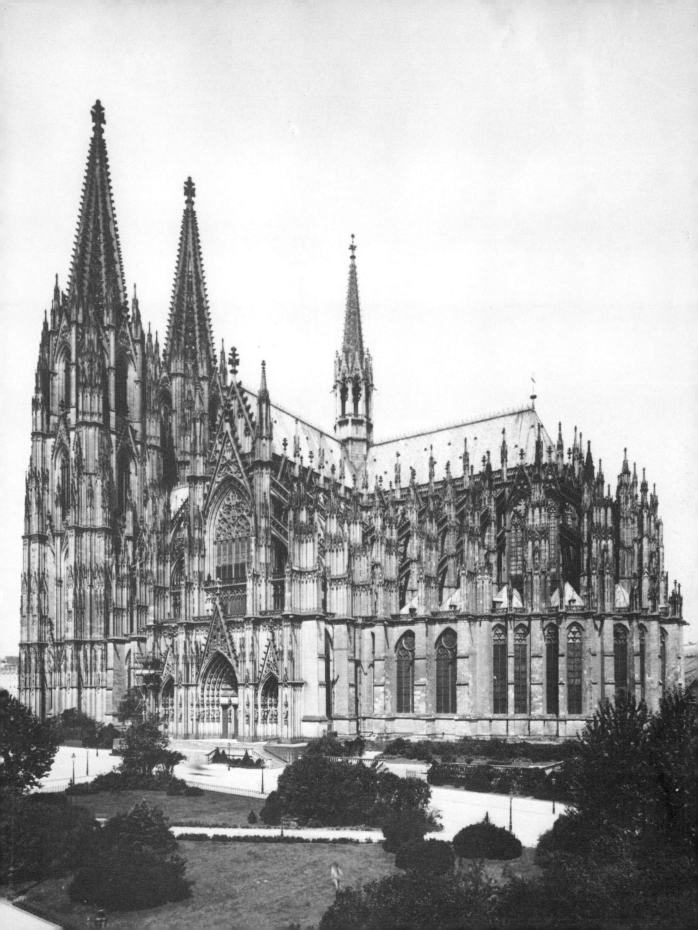

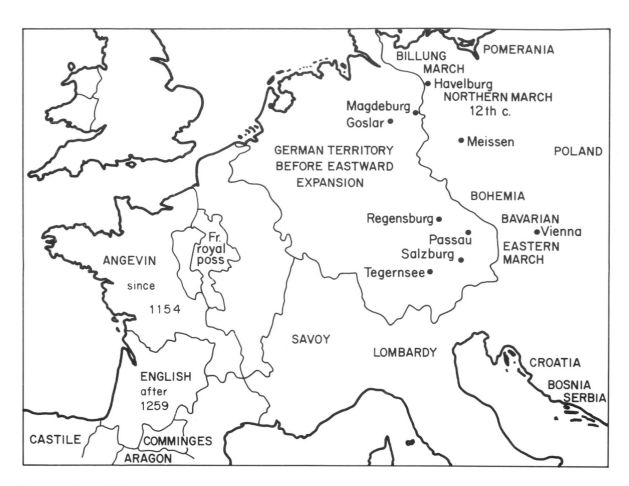

Western and central Europe from the twelfth to thirteenth centuries.

Bibliography

Baeuml, F.H. *Medieval Civilization in Germany 800–1273* Thames & Hudson, London, 1969.

Bishop, M. *The Penguin Book of the Middle Ages* Penguin, Harmondsworth, 1971.

Brooke, C. *The Structure of Medieval Society* Thames & Hudson, London, 1971.

Freising, Otto of *The Deeds of Frederick Barbarossa* Columbia University Press, New York, 1953.

Frenzel, H.A.U.E. *Daten Deutscher Dichtung* Vol.I Deutscher Taschenbuch Verlag, München, 1962.

Hay, D. *The Medieval Centuries* Methuen, London, 1953.

Munz, P. *Frederick Barbarossa, A Study in Medieval Politics* Eyre & Spottiswoode, London, 1969.

Pacaut, M. *Frederick Barbarossa* Collins, London, 1970.

Rowling, M. *Everyday Life in Medieval Times* Batsford, London, 1968.

Treharne, R.F. & H. Fullard *Muir's Atlas of Ancient, Medieval and Modern History* George Philip, London, 1982.

Ward, D. *The German Legends of the Brothers Grimm* Vols. I and II Millington, London, 1981.

GENEALOGY OF CHARACTERS

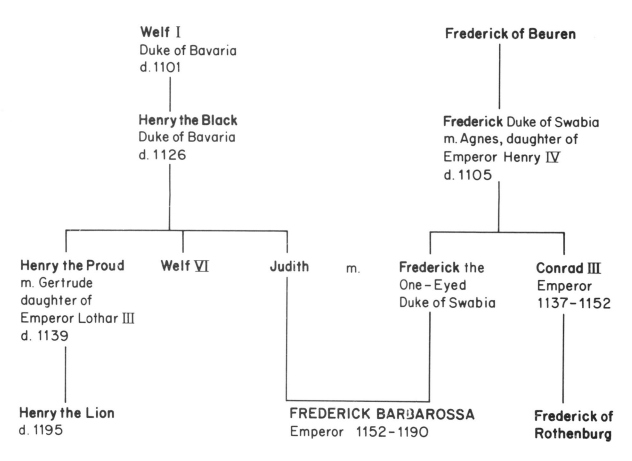

Welf I
Duke of Bavaria
d. 1101

Henry the Black
Duke of Bavaria
d. 1126

Henry the Proud
m. Gertrude
daughter of
Emperor Lothar III
d. 1139

Welf VI

Judith

Henry the Lion
d. 1195

FREDERICK BARBAROSSA
Emperor 1152-1190

Frederick of Beuren

Frederick Duke of Swabia
m. Agnes, daughter of
Emperor Henry IV
d. 1105

m.

Frederick the
One-Eyed
Duke of Swabia

Conrad III
Emperor
1137-1152

**Frederick of
Rothenburg**

Illustrations
Colour plates by James Field
Line illustrations by Chesca Potter
Maps and diagrams by Chartwell Illustrators
Photographs and other illustrations courtesy of: Bildarchiv Foto Marburg (pages 7, 23, 25, 29, 31, 33, 34, 37, 39, 41 and 45); Peter
Newark's Historical Pictures (page 35)

Index

Page numbers in *italics* refer to illustrations.